T0194416

GENESIS
AND
SCIENCE

SCIENCE VERIFIES CREATION AS TOLD IN GENESIS 1:1–27

BY EDMOND E. SHUMPERT

WESTBOW
PRESS®
A DIVISION OF THOMAS NELSON
& ZONDERVAN

Genesis 1:1-26 – 2 Peter 2:8 - Genesis 1:25,26 - Romans 14:5 and 10 – Genesis 1:25 – Genesis 1:1,2,3,5 – Genesis 1:6 – Genesis 1:9-12 – Genesis 1:14 and 16 – Genesis 1:20 and 22 – Genesis 1:24,25 and 26 – Genesis 1:1,2 and 3 – Genesis 4:16,17 and 25 – Genesis 1:20-26 – Genesis 2:8 – 1 Corinthians 15:40,43,40 - 1 Corinthians 15:1-8 - Luke 24:39 and 41 - John 1:1-14 – Genesis !:3 and 7 - Exodus 25:8 – Genesis 18:1,2 and 10 – Exodus 40:24,34,-39 -Phillipians 2:8 – quotes -The New American Standard Bible

WestBow Press books may be ordered through booksellers or by contacting:

WestBow Press
A Division of Thomas Nelson & Zondervan
1663 Liberty Drive
Bloomington, IN 47403
www.westbowpress.com
1 (866) 928-1240

ISBN: 978-1-9736-0991-9 (sc)
ISBN: 978-1-9736-0990-2 (e)

Print information available on the last page.

WestBow Press rev. date: 04/25/2019

To

Every Human Being

Contents

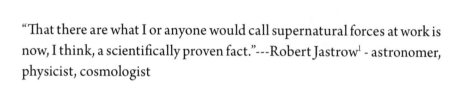

"That there are what I or anyone would call supernatural forces at work is now, I think, a scientifically proven fact."---Robert Jastrow[1] - astronomer, physicist, cosmologist

[1] Posted online by godevidence.com/2010/08/quotes-about-god/ - found in the ninth article down.

God, does not live in time, He is eternal, "The Existing One"; therefore, He can see all the things He created from the beginning of the universe to the present time as a blur of activity of six days, or, He can see them as a long drawn-out process of 13.7 billion years – whichever He pleases. And, since scientists have proven that God created the universe out of nothing, He could certainly create everything in Genesis 1:1-26 unimaginably rapidly in six days, six thousand years ago.—Edmond E. Shumpert 2016

INTRODUCTION

For many years I have thought, meditated and prayed about our problem with the proponents of Darwin's "Origin of Species", the so-called theory of evolution, which they claim to be a scientific fact as opposed to what they call the mythical scriptures in Genesis 1:1-26 and all the rest of the Bible.

Genesis 1: 1-26 is an amazing, complete, and beautiful synopsis on just one page. Therefore, Moses could not possibly have gone into much detail on any of the six days he describes. Because there is not much detail in any synopsis, each statement is very important. And when there is very little information in a scripture and later discoveries are made which can explain its meaning better, they can lead to the explanation of that scripture. There is one scripture in the New Testament which helps our understanding of creation, it is 2 Peter 2:8 where he explains God's mastery of time.

I think the best way we can find the needed agreement about Genesis 1: 25 and 26 is by deciding whether the interpretation of possible critics, or my interpretation is a better answer to the questions about these two scriptures. But when a discussion ends in disagreement, there can be disappointment, or anger, unfortunately. However, the apostle Paul answers how we can handle this problem in his New Testament letter to the Romans. Here are two of the verses in Romans 14: 5 and 10 - Verse 5 One man regards one day above another; another regards every day alike. Let each man be fully convinced in his own mind. Verse 10 But you, why do you judge your brother? Or you again, why do you regard your brother with contempt? For we will all stand before the judgment seat of God.

As predicted by the Lord, stumbling blocks will come, and a very large one is the "Origin of the Species" which was brought into the world by Charles Darwin and is being maintained by many people in the world. The question is, do Christians want to keep ignoring this stumbling block, or do we want to end it?

1

SCIENCE SUPPORTS GENESIS

In 1956, I was thirteen years old when I met a young fellow in my junior high school art class and it wasn't very long until we became good friends. This young man was a fairly intelligent guy and we enjoyed many discussions on various subjects. One day when I told him I was Christian he looked surprised and said he was an atheist. His brother was a college student who believed in Darwin's theory of evolution and had convinced my friend as a young fellow to be an atheist, too. When we were in high school he brought the subject of atheism up again and asked me what I thought of Darwin's theories. I answered him by saying that I thought scientists were only discovering how God created the universe. He replied that the universe has always existed and that all living things evolved into being by a series of accidental natural events. After high school we went our separate ways; I went to art school and he went to college. I always wished I could have given him better answers about God and creation, but all the scientists at that time seemed to agree that all animal life, including mankind, had accidentally evolved into being in "Darwin's warm little pond".

While reading Lee Strobel's book, "The Case for a Creator", I learned that many scientists who had always been atheists and others who had become atheists due to Darwinian propaganda in college shared with him that the scientific discoveries about the universe were a great help to them in realizing God's existence. For me, discovering the scientific and Biblical proofs in Lee Strobel's books has increased my faith to some extent and they improved my knowledge of the universe so that I have a better understanding of the whole Bible.

There are many of "the Lord's own" who are living now and will one day become believers from every group of people in the world. I have mainly written this book to help Christian high school and college students (or anyone else) to keep from being thrown off track by various sources of atheistic preaching of Darwin's myth of *natural creation* and perhaps spend many years without the Lord until they find their way to Him. As a young boy I was thrown off track when my family moved to a State with a far lower percentage of Christians per capita when compared to my birth State. We went to a number of churches when I was young man and I thought and sensed their members were misinformed and lacked the Love, the Spirit and the knowledge of our God and Savior Christ Jesus. This was also what I found as an adult. And I had to do the best I could with what I learned about the Lord from my Grandfather back home. These were tough years until I finally moved back to my home State. As a reader I would go to the library, and after a time I was talking with a library assistant who explained the Gospel to me. It must have been what I had heard before we moved away. Eight months later I fully received the Lord and was baptized at age 64! I had struggled for fifty-seven years. (I married the library assistant one year later!)

The first thing I would like to discuss is the *Creation*. Amazingly, it is written on just one page! All the scriptures in Genesis 1:1-26 are supported by scientific discoveries. And there are also a number of these scriptures whose meanings have been made clear by scientific findings. These will be discussed in Chapters two and three.

The first concept concerning the creation that we must realize is God "spoke" everything into existence – this has been verified by science, more on this later. The account of creation in Genesis 1:1-26 covers a vast number of things; however there seems to be one proof that is overlooked.—Moses didn't have any scientists to teach him, but with God to tell him the basic events of astronomy and earth science, he got it all correct! These verses of Genesis are quoted below, and each verse is followed by the science that verifies what it says. Occasionally there is a comment by me in this Comparison of science and Genesis 1:1-26. (All quotes of scripture in this book are from the New American Standard Bible).

Darwin's theory of evolution versus the "creation" has caused, perhaps, one of the biggest stumbling blocks in history. I believe the stumbling block of creation v. science disappears once we understand how all the scriptures are supported by scientific discoveries as explained in each chapter of this book. Now, let's begin comparing Genesis and Science on the first page of the Bible!

Genesis 1:1, 2, 3, 5
The First Day:
Genesis 1:1, 2, 3, 5 – 1 In the beginning God created the heavens and the earth. 2 The earth was formless and void, and darkness was over the deep, and the Spirit of God was moving over the surface of the waters. 3 Then God said, "Let there be light"....—5 God called the light day, and the darkness He called night.

(My comment)
Verse 1 The first thing God says is that He created the heavens – which, means the universe. Then He lists the earth after the heavens. Verse 2 He says that he created the earth as formless and void; and darkness was over the deep. Verse 3 God kindled the sun and it shone upon the earth.

Many people I have spoken with, about creation say "Let there be light" represents the beginning of the universe. But as I see in the scripture "Let there be light" has to be when the sun began to shine because verse 2 says there was darkness over the deep (ocean) – which means the earth was dark before the sun began to shine. This is verified by Verse 5 which says God called the light day, and the darkness He called night. This tells us there was day and night after He said "Let there be light". This sequence is the same as the scientific facts:

Scientific facts of the First Day: Verse 1 – 13.7 billion years ago God created the universe out of nothing.[1] Verse 2 - 4.5 billion years ago the earth was covered with water. (There was water, instead of ice, on the earth due to the temperature of its surface at that time).[2] Verse 3 - 3.6 billion years ago the sun began to shine.[3] This means the earth had water 1 billion years before the sun began to shine. Hence, scientific theory supports Genesis 1:1, 2 and 3 - end of first day. (13.7 billion years is how scientists see time. This is explained in Chapter 2)

"On or about 8/27/14 - I found on the internet, a Stanford Solar Center chart that stated the sun began to shine 3.6 billion years ago".

The Second Day:
Genesis 1:6; - 6 God said, "Let there be clear sky in the midst of the waters"

Science of the second day: At that time the earth's surface temperature must have been fairly hot; therefore, there was a space of clear air between the warm water of the ocean and the water in the sky - which formed a complete cloud cover. (Venus still has a complete cloud cover. Somehow Venus still has a surface temperature of 850 degrees). Science supports Genesis 1:6 - end of second day.

The Third Day:
Genesis 1:9, 10, 11, and 12; - 9 Then God said, "Let the waters below heaven be gathered into one place, and let the dry land appear"; and 10 "He called the waters seas". 11 Then God said, "Let the earth sprout forth vegetation", and, 12 "The earth brought forth vegetation".

Science of the Third Day - (part 1) Genesis 1:9 and 10: "Let the dry land appear" - This means there was one continental mass: Let us start with asteroids.[4] Asteroids are usually metallic or rock, metal, other elements, and water. A large conglomerated asteroid (made of rock, metals and other elements) must have arrived at least 4 billion years ago on earth; and this formed the original super-continent called Pangaea;[5] Scientists say that the earth's surface was very hot in its beginning. The earth's heat probably melted this gigantic asteroid over part of the earth. This is because the earth was not hot enough to make it flow out over its entire crust; (for the sources of all these scientific concepts see the footnotes at the end of this chapter). Listed below is the scientific time-line from the arrival of the original continent to its emerging from the ocean which previously covered the entire earth:

1—Approximately 4 billion years ago a gigantic asteroid deposited the materials that formed the continental mass on the earth and they were melted partially over the crust.

2—There are still "clouds" of ice balls and ice crystals traveling through space. This provided much of the water found on earth. 4 billion years ago the earth's water covered the entire earth and the original continental layer; there was much more water on the earth at its beginning.

3—After much water evaporated from the earth and it had cooled, snow and ice formed on the poles and mountains after the one super-continent (of science and Genesis 1:9-12) emerged; thereby, the waters were "gathered in one place and the dry land appeared". Thus, earth science verifies Genesis 1:9 and 10.

NOTE: The original super continent (pangaea) began to break apart in the early Jurassic period (200 million years ago). How could Moses know the earth was covered with water on the first day when he wrote this about the first day in Verse 2 "...the Spirit of God was moving over the surface of the waters." This means the earth was covered with water. And how did he know there was only one continent when he wrote on the second day, "Let the waters below heaven be gathered into one place, and let the dry land appear." This means there was only one continent because it was in one place and the water in the other place. Science says three things about the water and the dry land: 1—The earth was sufficiently cooled to be covered with water. [In Moses' vision] 2—The water was blasted off by the sun until methane evaporated from the land and protected the atmosphere from the sun's rays. 3—One super-continent (pangaea) therefore, emerged from the water.

Science of the third day - (part 2) Genesis 1:11 and 12 11 Then God said, "Let the earth sprout forth vegetation". And, 12 "The earth brought forth vegetation". The sun was already in the sky; and by the latter part of the third day the earth had cooled enough for the vegetation to grow. Thus these two verses are self-explanatory and are verified by scientific theory - end of third day.

The Fourth Day:
Genesis 1:14, 16; - 14 Then God said, "Let there be lights in the expanse of the heavens to separate the day from the night" and 16 God made the two lights, the greater light [sun] to govern the day and the lesser light [moon] to govern the night; He made the stars, also".

(My Comment) Note that God said "lights". This is to indicate that He added a second light - the moon; and in verse 16 where He said, "two lights", God simply reiterated what He said about the sun in Genesis 1:5 - "God called the light day". So, verse 14 does not mean that He created the sun on the fourth day; nor, does verse 16 mean that He created the stars on the fourth day just because it says, "He made the stars, also". This statement by Moses reads as though it was an after-thought, as one might make in a synopsis. Mentioning the stars on the first day would have been an unnecessary distraction from the main point being made. The sun is also mentioned on the fourth day, but it was not created on the fourth day, either.

Science of the fourth day: The moon's orbit is at a very different angle to all the planets, therefore the moon must have entered our solar system from some other part of the universe at a time long after the planets formation in the same orbital plane as the protoplanetoid disc. The moon's orbit is more elliptical than the planets' orbits (typical of a younger orbit).[6] And, the weight (mass) of the moon must have greatly changed the angle of the earth's axis. Thus the arrival of the moon was after the continental mass and water.

(My comment): If God had not added the moon, the earth's axis would have swung wildly and made the earth uninhabitable].[7] Scientific theory supports Genesis 1: 14, 16 - end of the fourth day.

The Fifth Day:
Genesis 1:20, 22; - 20 Then God said "Let the waters team with swarms of living creatures" and, 22 God blessed them, saying, "Be fruitful and multiply, and fill the waters in the seas, and let the birds multiply on the earth". These two verses are self-explanatory.

Science of the fifth day: The appearance of animals happened at a logical time and in accordance with scientific findings. Scientists have determined that all the major animal types appeared in the Cambrian era. Darwin, himself, said that if science finds that none of the major types of animal fossils existed before the Cambrian era, his theory would be proven wrong. Science has discovered that there were no major animal fossils before the Cambrian era. - end of fifth day.

The Sixth Day:
Genesis 1: 24, 25 and 26
Verse 24 says, Then God said, "Let the earth bring forth living creatures after their kind; cattle and creeping things and beasts of the earth after their kind; and it was so." Verse 25 says, "God made the beasts of the earth after their kind, and the cattle after their kind, and *everything that creeps on the ground* after its kind; and God saw that it was good." Verse 26 says - Then God said, *"Let Us make man in Our Image"*, according to Our likeness; and let them rule over the fish of the sea and over the birds of the sky and over the cattle and over all the earth, and over every creeping thing that creeps on the earth."

The sixth day of creation will need such a lengthy discussion that it will be in chapter 2. There, I will go into my interpretation of the anthropological and theological meanings of these three verses of Genesis 1:1-26.

NOTES

1   Google – From Wikipedia the free encyclopedia – Reference "The World Factbook". www.cia.gov. Retrieved 2016-03-17. We quote, "There exist numerous more or less mutually compatible hypotheses as to how water may have accumulated on Earth's surface over the past 4.6 billion years in sufficient quantity to form oceans." Also: "Origin of water on the earth" - www.smithsonianmag.com/.../ how-didwater-come-to-earth-72037248/ See also our own theory of how the earth formed in the note in "Earth and Planets" below. Quote from article by Brian Greene - Smithsonian Magazine - May 2013 – (Third paragraph from bottom) "Both comets and asteroids can contain ice. And if, by colliding with Earth, they added the amount of material some scientists suspect, such bodies could easily have delivered oceans' worth of water. Accordingly, each has been fingered as a suspect in the mystery."

2   Google - "Age of the Earth" – Wikipedia free encyclopedia-reference- "Age of the Earth". - U.S. Geological Survey. 1997. Archived from the original on 23 December 2005. Retrieved 2006-01-10. The U.S. Geological survey indicates that the earth is 4.5 billion years old. See our ideas about The Solar System, Earth, and Planets below these footnotes.

3   Google - "How old is the Sun, and when did it start to shine?" Several websites indicate that the sun is @ 4.5 billion years old. On the solar-center.stanford. edu/ FAQ /Qage.html (date not given) a Stanford Solar Center article by Amara Graps states the following in paragraph five: "What is meant by "luminous?" We mean that the Sun was at or near the stable part of its lifetime called the "main sequence" more than 3.6 billion years ago." And, on or before 8/26/14, I also saw a Stanford Solar Center chart that indicated the sun began to shine 3.6 billion years ago.

4   Asteroids: What are asteroids made of? By SPACE.com Staff | March 1, 2012 12:53pm ET - "Asteroids are made of rock, metals and other elements. Some even contain water, astronomers say. Asteroids that are mostly stone sometimes are more like loose piles of rubble. Asteroids that are mostly iron are more rock-solid."

5   Google - Pangaea - Wikipedia, the free encyclopedia https://en.wikipedia.org/ wiki/Pangaea. NOTE: We could not find any statement on Google by scientists of where Pangaea originated. The arrival of a gigantic comet is one concept of how Pangaea formed on earth. Our logic is that if all the materials of the continents were part of the original earth, these materials would have been so hot that they would have flowed over the entire surface of the earth, and thus the ocean would cover the whole earth - making almost all life forms impossible.

6   oon's orbit: Orbit of the Moon quoted From the Milankovich Cycles - Wikipedia, the free encyclopedia – 7/3/16. "The orbit of the Moon is distinctly elliptical, with an average eccentricity of 0.0549." and at present the Earth's orbit's eccentricity is "0.017 and decreasing."—This quote is found under the title – "Orbit's Shape (eccentricity)" in this article.

7   Quote from the Milankovich Cycles – "Axial Tilt (Obliquity)" - Wikipedia, the free encyclopedia – 1/13/16. Earth's axis [tilt] would have swung wildly: "Scientists using computer models to study more extreme tilts than those that actually occur have concluded that climate extremes at high obliquity would be particularly threatening to advanced forms of life that presently exist on Earth. They noted that high obliquity would not likely sterilize a planet completely, but would make it harder for fragile, warmblooded land-based life to thrive as it does today."—

2

GENESIS, SCIENCE AND MAN

Great news inadvertently began to unfold for Christianity in 1915. Albert Einstein developed his theory of general relativity and started applying it to the whole universe. He was shocked to discover that it was not eternal. His equations showed it was either exploding or imploding. From Aristotle's time, 350BC all the way to 1965, it was believed that the universe was eternal; thus all the Galaxies and stars always stayed in the same place in the heavens.

In the early 1920s, Russian mathematician Alexander Freidman and Belgian astronomer George Lemaitre created a model on Einstein's theory. Thus, they believed the universe was expanding (exploding). Astronomer Fred Hoyle derisively called this the "Big Bang"—because it meant that the universe had a beginning, thus, it had to have a transcendent Creator.

In 1929, Edwin Hubble discovered that light coming to us from distant galaxies appeared redder than it should be, and that this is a universal feature of galaxies in all parts of the sky. This allowed him to reason that the universe was flying apart at enormous velocities. This verified Freidman and Lemaitre's model that indicated the universe was expanding.

During the 1940s, George Gamow predicted that if the "Big bang" really happened, the background temperature of the universe should be just a few degrees above absolute zero. In 1965, two scientists accidentally discovered that the background radiation of the universe is about 3.7 degrees above absolute zero.

The last piece of evidence for the "Big Bang" is the origin of light elements in the 1940s. Heavy elements like iron and carbon are synthesized at 600,000 degrees in the interior of stars and exploded through supernovae into space. Light elements like deuterium and helium cannot be synthesized in the interior of stars; they would need temperatures that were billions of degress and to be produced in the "Big Bang" itself, in the early stage of the creation of the universe 13.7 billion years ago.

(The five paragraphs above are the scientific history of the universe, found in "The Case for a Creator", page 105, by Lee Strobel, 2004).

NOTE: The term "Big Bang" may have been derisive but the discovery of the actual event gave proof of what Moses wrote in Genesis 1: 1, 2 and 3:

Verse 1 the Big Bang represents the moment the universe began its existence, as stated in verse 1 - In the beginning God created the "*heavens*" - which means the universe; space, galaxies, and the stars— these, and the *earth* are the first things God told Moses in verse 1.

>My comment: The light of the universe was too far away to "light" the earth as in day and night. —

Verse 2 Moses writes that the earth was formless and void, there was "darkness over the deep" and God's Spirit was over the water.

>My comment: The sun was not shinning at this time.

Verse 3 God says, "Let there be light" - this is when He kindled the sun's light, thus it shone on earth. Then "God called the light day, and the darkness He called night."

>My comment:There is another crucial point: many theologians say that the flash of light in verse 3 is the beginning of the universe. When we

look closely, we see that when God created the "heavens", He created the universe! The flash of light was when the sun began to cause day and night! There was no more darkness over the deep (the ocean) – at the end of verse 1. (The order of all these things is confirmed by science – see chapter1).

I have heard a few Christians say the universe did not come from a huge explosion. I think it is better to say that God can create the universe any way He pleases. As for an explosion, when there is nothing existing, it doesn't hurt anyone if God creates a gigantic explosion. In fact, God created all the physics for the natural world; so chemistry, biology and life all were made possible by this explosion. This explosion is implied by Moses' words in Genesis 1: 1 which say - "...God created the heavens..." - which means He created the universe - perhaps Moses saw a vision of the Creation - shown and told to him by the Lord.

When one mixes Genesis and Science, there will be controversy:
I have disagreed with a few people about certain verses in the Bible that do not have a clear explanation of details which potentially have meanings that are very important, and yet we can find agreement by deciding whether their, or my interpretation answers the questions about the scriptures better. But when a discussion is irreconcilable, it can end with disappointment, or anger, unfortunately. However, the apostle Paul answers how we can handle this problem in his New Testament letter to the Romans. The following are the verses I have selected in Romans 14: 5 and 10 - Verse 5 One man regards one day above another; another regards every day alike. Let each man be fully convinced in his own mind. Verse 10 But you, why do you judge your brother? Or you again, why do you regard your brother with contempt? For we will all stand before the judgment seat of God.

Some people say that fossils and other scientific data are forged. There have been a number of fossils and data that have been exposed as forgeries, but that doesn't prove all fossils and data are forged. When forgeries are rejected and other fossils are found to be undeniably genuine, this indicates that there is a good degree of policing of scientific discoveries.

If the scientists were dishonest, they could have destroyed and discontinued the research on Einstein's theory of relativity, which they feared would have refuted their atheistic beliefs. Scientists knew that Einstein's equations showed the universe was either exploding or imploding. If the universe was imploding it would be doomed and not eternal (they believed it was eternal); and if it was exploding, that means that it had a beginning and an end (as Jews and Christians believe). Atheistic scientists also knew "anything that begins to exist has a cause". Be that as it may, these honest scientists continued working on Einstein's theory of general relativity, and they were very upset when empirical evidence proved that the universe was exploding; this meant it had a beginning, and that its cause was a transcendent God who created the universe.

During the last five decades large numbers of scientists have become believers; such as Albert Einstein, Allan Sandage, Robert Jastrow, Paul Davies, Arno Penzias, John Polkinghorn, Nikola Tesla, Werner Heisenberg, and many others.

MY THOUGHTS ON GOD'S MASTERY OF TIME:

When questioning what scientists say about time as told in Genesis 1: 1-26, the first thing Christians will probably ask is, "How can the universe be 13.7 billion years old when the Bible says the creation was 6,000 years ago?" My concept below is actually an expansion of the Apostle Peter's statement in 2 Peter 2: 8 - "But let this one fact not escape your notice, beloved, that with the Lord one day is as a thousand years, and a thousand years as one day."

How Was the Universe Created in Six Days, 6,000 years ago?

Since Genesis says that the universe was created in six days, we have to acknowledge each day has trillions of things that were created in each twenty-four hour period of those six days. This can only mean that God created trillions of things very rapidly during six days by speaking them into existence. Again, God does not exist in time; He is eternal. Therefore, He can see all the things He created from the beginning of the universe to the present time as a blur of activity of six days, or He can see them as a long drawn-out process of 13.7 billion years – whichever He pleases. And, since scientists have proven that God created the universe out of nothing, He could certainly create everything in Genesis extremely rapidly in a blur of six days, six thousand years ago.

By acknowledging the six day creation, Bible scholars are saying that "trillions" of things were created very rapidly in each day. What I have recognized is that scientists have discovered that there are far more things created than the Bible scholars of the past knew about when they interpreted the Bible before all these things were discovered. The place where their interpretations of the creation in Genesis 1:25 differ with mine is that I am willing to add the *undeniable* things the scientists have discovered in the past fifty years, and many of today's scholars and the believers who follow them, are not. (There will be a lot written on Genesis 1:25 in chapters 2 and 3). Again, the way the scientist and all the rest of us see the passing of time, does not mean that God is limited in how rapidly He can create things in a six day period. In fact, God created time by setting the universe into motion and giving the power of conscientiousness and thought to us. Motion is why there is time in the "natural" universe; and the faster the acts of creation the more things can be created in a given time. Thus, to understand both Genesis and Science we must realize that the earth is 6,000 years old and 4.5 billion years old at the same time. This is the case because all the years of what scientists call epochs are compressed into twenty-four hours of each day of the six days of creation, but the evidence that is laid down in the earth and the universe looks like billions of years to the scientists - and to us. And, let us remember that Peter said, "...to the Lord one day is as a thousand years and a thousand years is as one day"!

Since the discovery that the universe was created out of nothing, there have been enormous discoveries in the natural sciences! Please read on—

Before I Talk about Natural Science I have to say this: There are a good number of convincing proofs that Darwin's theory of evolution is not science; it is a myth. For one thing, there is scientific evidence that not even one living cell could have evolved into being as Darwin claims. Evolution can only occur in living organisms that God has already created.

And, contrary to what Darwin seems to claim—humans are not related to apes and/or monkeys. The following used to be a hot button subject between Christians and Darwinists, but this is fading out. Please let me quote Jonathan Wells, PhD, PhD; he said, "If you assume, as neo-Darwinism does, that we are a product of our genes, then you are saying that the dramatic differences between us and chimpanzees are due to two percent of our genes." he replied. "The problem is that the so-called body building genes are in the ninety-eight percent. The two percent of genes that are different are really rather trivial genes that have little to do with anatomy. So the supposed similarity of DNA in humans and chimpanzees is a problem for neo-Darwinism right there.

"Second, it's not surprising when you look at two organisms that are similar anatomically, you often find they're similar genetically. Not always; there's a striking discordance with some organisms. But does this prove common ancestry?

He shook his head as he answered his own question: "No, it's just as compatible with common design as it is with common ancestry. A designer might very well decide to use common building materials to create different organisms, just as builders use the same materials— steel girders, rivets, and so forth—to build different bridges that end up looking very dissimilar from one another."—Quote from Lee Strobel's, "The Case for a Creator", pages 54-55 - 2004 - Zondervan. In answer to questions by Lee Strobel,

Now, I will discuss the scientists' methods of finding and dating fossils:

How do scientists find fossils?

They decide what kind of fossils they want to find. Next they consult a geographic map of the surface of the earth made by geologists of the past. This helps them to determine if the rock they're looking for is exposed. Then they get permission to be on the land and they systematically start walking the surface looking for hints of fossils. Fossils are also sometimes found by accident, like the mammoths that were found in Colorado recently. A crew was excavating for a house and stumbled on the fossils.[2]

How do scientists date fossils and artifacts?

For relatively recent fossils and artifacts, dating by carbon 14 is the most accurate method. For older fossils it is necessary to analyze the geological layer in which they are found; fossils and artifacts located in an undisturbed geological layer of a certain age are the same age as the layer in which they are found, necessarily. They compare the substances in newly found stone and embedded fossils with known dated layers of the earth. Artifacts are tools, weapons, pottery, etc., usually dated by human remains found with them and by the geological layers in which they are found. Both fossils and artifacts can also be compared to substances embedded in the one mile thick layer of ice from Greenland.[3]

My Comments:

I have heard some people say that all the fossils are hoaxes. I am a sculptor and I know how impossible it would be to fake the interior of a simple bone. For one thing, you would have to make untold thousands of minuscule sponge-like chambers and with holes and tunnels for nerves and blood vessels running through some parts of them and by working on the bone from the inside out. Besides all that, you would have to put DNA in the bone! Furthermore, all this would have to match the structure of real bones perfectly. And sometimes I hear that the dating of fossils is also forged. My knowledge of science tells me there are many ways to establish the age of fossils that make sense to me. And you can cross-check them with the various other methods of dating; more on this later.

I have seen many fossils in museums. One was a dinosaur fossil. It was a chunk of solid rock five feet long, four feet wide, and over two feet thick with thousands of fingernail size scales all over its surface—it was absolutely beautiful. This was a piece of actual solid rock with a very detailed imprint of the skin with wrinkles at the back side of the "armpit" that fanned out toward the shoulder and front part of the back. The only way this imprint could be on a chunk of rock would be that animal went through a series of geological downs and ups in the manner fossils are most often formed in the earth. They were buried by mud slides, volcanic ash, or sunk in bogs, or tar pits. Once they were covered by one of these situations, they were buried deeper and deeper because these "burial" places are at the lower levels of the land where sediments could form, so they went down until they were under tremendous pressure. The fossilization process varies according to external conditions and tissue type. The various types of fossilization processes include permineralization, bioimmuration, adpression, replacement and recrystallization, casts and molds. When the fossil containing sedments rise back up to the surface of the land, erosion exposes them or the characteristic of fossil beds; and perhaps a scientist finds them. A fake rock replicating this process and being acceptable is completely out of the question! As I recall, this dinosaur fossil was at the Metropolitan Museum in New York in 1965. (Permineralization, etc.- From Wikipedia, the free encyclopedia-1/6/19).

I have spoken with some people who think there is no undeniable evidence of fossils and remains over 6,000 years old because the Bible says the earth is 6,000 years old. I answer their assertion by telling them about my explanation of how the Universe can be 13.7 billion years old and 6,000 years old at the same time (See above). They are thinking about Adam's age and not considering all the other things that God created very rapidly during the first five and a half days of creation and not realizing that Adam was created in the last half of the sixth day of creation. And please remember what Paul said in Romans 14: 5 and 10. See my thoughts above about God's mastery of time and the scientists' earth bound perception of time!

The undeniable evidence of proto-man remains as they relate to the Bible:

Let Us Look at Some Undeniable Fossils and Skeletons Found by Scientists: I have selected five sources. These sources have been studied and verified to be authentic remains, fossils and artifacts. One of the most recent findings of "proto-man" remains are those of the five Dmanisi Georgicus skulls and other skeletal parts. There is convincing scientific proof that they are 1.8 million years old – in the way scientists analyze and calculate time.

Here are five examples:

1—The five excellent skulls and several other bones of the 1.8 million year old fossils of Dmanisi Georgicus. Homo Georgicus is a species of Homo that was proposed in 2002. It is based on fossil skulls and jaws found in Dmanisi, Georgia in 1999 and 2001 – see photos on Google.[4]

2—Oldest human DNA from a 400,000 yr old skeleton found in Spain.

Scientists have found the oldest DNA evidence yet of humans' biological history...In a paper in the journal Nature, scientists reported Wednesday that they had retrieved ancient human DNA from a fossil dating back about 400,000 years.[5]

3—30,000 old "Cro-Magnon"— *"Cro-Magnon" Early Humans (Cro-Magnon Man)* Cro-magnon skull Prehistoric modern humans—were essentially modern homo sapiens. They created paintings and sculptures, wore jewelry, made musical instruments and used dozens of different kinds of implements including tools. Cro-Magnon men were named after a French rock shelter discovered in 1968. Homo sapien means "discerning man." [Source Rick Gore, National Geographic, September 1997, and John Pfieffer, Smithsonian magazine, October 1986]

Also "Cro-Magnon - Size : males: 5 feet 9 inches, 143 pounds; females: 5 feet 3 inches, 119 pounds. Brain size and body features: the same as people today; *Skull Features:* slightly bigger teeth and slightly thicker skulls than people today. Source - Google 11-23-18 at factsanddetails. com/world/cat56/sub361/item1474.html[6]

4—9,000-year-old Neolithic City Discovered in Jerusalem Valley. People were still transitioning from hunting-gathering to farming when this vast town with stone houses and red-floored gathering sites arose by Jerusalem, and finally, began to appreciate children. Story - By Nir Hasson and Ruth Schuster Jul 16, 2018 Haaretz Israel News.[7]

5—Neanderthal in all of us!

Neanderthals are an extinct species of human who died out around 30,000 years ago. However, Neanderthals, being the lesser number, interbred with the larger numbered Cro-Magnon, thus it is extremely possible that the small amount of variation in the Neanderthal genome may have been wiped out by the modern human genome. Almost all Europeans have a small amount of Neanderthal DNA of 30,000 years ago. This is proof of what I call "proto-man" who lived before 6,000 years ago.[8]

Why do I call these creatures proto-man? The prefix "Proto" means – lower, ancient, primordial. They were a series of rough models created before God made Adam - the "first man" in His image! Just because the DNA is almost identical does not make them the same as the man Adam. I call them proto-man because they are far from what God calls "Man".

Now, let us look at some very important verses in Genesis:
Genesis 1: 1 – 26 is an extremely short, brilliant, complete synopsis of a huge number of things and events! To me this means every *verse* and every

word is extremely important to our understanding of God's creation of everything in the universe!.

Let us look at three extremely significant Bible verses on the sixth day of creation. I will quote the first two verses from the first half of the Sixth Day of Creation: Genesis 1: 24, 25

Verse 24 says - Then God said, "Let the earth bring forth living creatures after their kind; cattle and creeping things and beasts of the earth after their kind; and it was so." Verse 25 says, "God made the beasts of the earth after their kind, and the cattle after their kind, and *everything that creeps on the ground* after its kind; and God saw that it was good".—This verse is the time wherein proto-man was created.

Now I quote verse 26 which tells us what happened in the second half of The Sixth Day of creation.

Verse 26 says - Then God said, *"Let Us make man in Our Image,* according to Our likeness....".

Someone asked me a question about the last part of Genesis 1:26 in which God speaks of Adam and Eve and their descendants saying, *"...let them rule...over every creeping thing that creeps on the earth."* This person's question was "Will Adam and Eve and and their descendants rule over every creeping thing including proto-man?" God gave Adam and Eve a powerful command not to eat of the "Tree of Good and Evil"; and by eating of it they and their descendants fell from paradise. Thus, whatever they would have done after "the fall" is up for speculation.

What is the importance of these verses!
As a young student I found anthropology and palaeontology very interesting even though I didn't believe in Darwin's theory of evolution. Nevertheless, over the years I have read every article that I came across about prehistoric anthropological fossils, remains, artifacts, villages and towns on all continents. I am pleased with, and enthused about what

21

has been found and may be found in the numerous twenty-first century discoveries and excavations.

The debate between Darwinist scientists and the Bible scholars started one hundred and fifty years ago. Naturally, the Bible scholars were upholding the 6,000 year old creation, as opposed to Darwin's theory of billions of years of evolution. Public school college professors, the National News Media, and some magazine publishers are still peddling the dis-proven Darwin theory of the "Origin of Species". Thus, we have an uphill battle.

Look at the change in the United States in regard to the decline of the percentage of people who are Christians. I think this is largely due to our Bible scholars' inability to explain how the discovery of the undeniable ancient proto-man remains fit into Genesis 1:1-26. The Church is speading the gospel around the world; however, there are many people in Europe and North America who have been turned away for many years by Darwin's Stumbling Block – the myth of evolution.

The following paragraph proves my interpretation is correct by using the method of "the inference to the best explanation" of the creation of proto-man as in Genesis 1: 25:

First we must remember my thouhgts on God's mastery of time (based on 2 Peter 2:8).—To God the universe can be 13.7 billion years old and 6,000 years old at the same time. He can see His creation of everything in a blur of activity of six days or He can see His creation in a long drawn out process of 13.7 billion years. But due to their atheism some scientists are thrilled to find great fossils of proto-man and use them against the Bible. Let them say what they will, Moses gave us Genesis 1: 25 – which is the verse that says *"everything that creeps on the ground"* was created - and that it was good. Therefore, this verse means that every land creature *(including proto-man)* was created during the first part of the Sixth Day. Then Moses gave us Genesis 1: 26 – where it says, Then God said, "Let Us create man in Our image." This is where God created Adam. And, of course, He gave Adam a spirit, a moral conscience, conscietiousness, and *ETERNAL LIFE!* Thus, the difference between Adam and *proto-man* is almost as much as the difference between ALIVE and *DEAD—Adam was created in God's image having eternal life—Proto-man died and turned to dust! Proto-man was scattered here and there over the earth—Adam was created in the "Garden of Eden" - which was the beginning of God's plan for mankind in His image!*

Please allow me to submit an analogy here:
There were a number of designs, working models and even moving vehicles made before what mankind calls the "first car" - examples of "proto-car" 60 AD to 1770 AD: 1—In 60 AD an ancient Greek drew a picture of his design for a motorized chariot. 2—In 1267, Ferdinand Verbiest built a small model of a turbine-steam-powered car. 3—In 1770 Nicolas Joseph Cugnot made a steam tractor. It could only go two miles per hour.(8) Due to lacking certain attributes, these proto-car designs did not come up to what mankind considers to be an automobile. The "first car" was made by Mercedes Benz in 1885. It could speed along at 12 miles per hour and carry a passenger.(9) Proto-man was not given a spirit, a moral conscience, or eternal life. Lacking these attributes, God did not call any of them the "first man" because they were not made in His image. As stated above, God gave Adam a spirit, moral conscience, and eternal life – but due to Adam and Eve's sin, they and all of humanity lost their eternal life. (See "God sent Jesus to atone for our sins" in chapter 4). NOTE: the Cugnot tractor and Mercedes' "first car" can be seen on Google.(9)

A Few More Words on the Six Days of Creation:
No matter what our interpretation is, I need to make one thing perfectly clear; God said that the heavens and the earth were created in six days; and this is what we Christians believe. We assert that the Bible is true. However, atheists and some scientists are still preaching Darwin's false theory of evolution v. creation, and thereby a stumbling block that Darwin brought into the world is being maintained by many scientists and government school educators. The question is, do Christians want to continue this stumbling block or do we want to end it? The Apostle

Paul tells us not to wrangle over words. We need to be patient, kind, understanding, knowledgeable, loving, and as agreeable as possible without compromising or denying God's Word and the true, verifiable, factual discoveries of science. We all need to study Genesis and Science to understand them, instead of assuming we know exactly what Genesis means whether we are Christians, Jews, scientists or others. We must also refrain from, and reject, specious arguments. And if we find there are things we cannot understand we must pray and believe that God will give us the answers in His time.

As stated above, Scientists, anthropologists, and archaeologists have discovered many fossils and skeletons that were embedded in hundreds, thousands, and millions of yearly layers under the earth's surface. They have also found cities and villages that are much older than six thousand years. This scientific evidence indicates that there was a type of "proto-man" living far longer that six thousand years ago (as scientists reckon time). These proto-man were not created in God's image. To deny that these creatures were on earth before 6,000 years ago is as damaging to the Bible's credibility as a doctrine that insists the sun travels around the earth each day – when in fact the earth travels around the sun in 365 1/4 days. Furthermore, the fact that God said He created "everything that creeps on the ground" in the Genesis 1:25 is another indication that there was a proto-man creature living before 6,000 years ago. And, because Adam was the *"first man"* made in God's image the Bible correctly calls him the *"first man"*. The concept of a proto-man does not change a word that Moses wrote and makes creation clearer to all our minds and removes this stumbling block.'

NOTES

1   Scientific history found in, "The Case for a Creator", page 105, by Lee Strobel, 2004.

2   :https//morgridge.org/blue-sky/how-do-scientists-find-fossils Found Google 11-23-18

3   :https//morgridge.org/blue-sky/how-do-scientists-find-fossils Found Google 11-23-18

4   1.8 million year old Dmanisi Georgicus. Homo georgicus – Simple English Wikipedia, the free wikipedia.org/wiki/Homo_georgicus

5   400,000 year old humanoid in Spain. See the evidence-this website—*"400,000 year old human DNA found in Spain – Hang The Bankers"* https://hangthebankers. com/400000-years-old-human-dna-found-in-spain Source:http://www:nytimes. com/2013/12/05/science/at-400000-years-oldest-human-dna-yet-found-raises-new-mysteries.html

6   30,000 old *"Cro-Magnon"*

7   More on 9,000 year old village in Israel. Google 11-20-18 9,000 year old Neolithic city discovered in Jerusalem... https://**www.haaretz.com**/archaeology/. premium.MAGAZINE-**9-000-year**... Flint tools found in **9,000-year old** Neolithic **village**, Motza Emil Salman Domestic houses in which the hoi polloi lived didn't have particularly invested flooring beyond dirt or basic plaster. The public places in prehistoric Motza had better plastering, colored red, Khalaily says.

8   *Neanderthal in all of us! Neanderthals are an extinct species of human who died out around 30,000 years ago. Evidence suggests that Neanderthals were cultured in ways very similar to how modern humans are today. Apparently the Neanderthals, being the lesser number, it is extremely possible that the small amount of variation in the Neanderthal genome may have been wiped out by the modern human genome. The SciHawk: The Neanderthos in all of us – The Seahawk https://theseahawk.org*

9   "Proto-cars": 1—60 AD Greek "car" 2—Verbiest's turbine-steam-powered "car" 3—Cugnot steam tractor - "First car" - 4—Mercedes Benz 1885 "the first car" - photos can be found on Google.

3

GENESIS, SCIENCE AND MANKIND

Bill Nye "the Science Guy" (a promoter of Darwinian evolution) criticized some Christians for trying to prove the earth is 6,000 years old. In a Newsmax interview Mr. Nye said, "But whatever you believe, whatever deity or higher power you might believe in, the earth is not 6,000 years old." Mr. Nye also said;

"School children taught creationism will not be able to participate in the future like children taught evolution because they will not have this fundamental idea that you can question things, you can think critically, and you can use skeptical thought to learn about nature." And He said;

"The problem is we have adults who have very strong, conservative views that are reluctant to let kids learn about evolution," Nye said, citing "people who get on school boards and want to introduce doubt about the main idea in biology."[1]

But, I say, that children will not learn to think critically, or question things, if the only theory taught to them about nature is Darwinism. Mr. Nye is also forgetting that scientists have discovered the fact of the Big Bang cosmology. This means they have discovered that the universe was created out of nothing! Scientific reasoning about nature says that "Whatever begins to exist has a cause". And, since the universe came out of nothing, most scientists are now saying that a transcendental cause outside of nature created the universe.[2]

And as a matter of fact, it is Mr. Nye who is trying to stifle critical thinking about evolution which is not the only idea about nature. Actually, since it has been discovered that it is impossible for a living cell to develop by accident on the earth's surface or in it's waters, Darwin's theory of the "Origin of Life" is invalidated (see the four paragraphs below). Nor was there a gradual evolution of the species before the Cambrian Era. It has also been discovered that a vast array of almost all the animal body types began to exist all at once at the beginning of the Cambrian Era. This kills Darwin's "Tree of Evolution".

Teaching Children About Nature, Science and God:
For anything at all to exist there has to be something that is eternal; and since we know it is not the universe, it is the Creator who is eternal. It is He who does not have a cause that is found in nature. Therefore truly educated children should be taught about nature, science and God. They need to know that there is also an eternal Creator beyond and greater than nature if they are to have a clue to understanding their world! And since Judaism and Christianity have taught that God created the universe out of nothing for the past 3,500 and 2,000 years, respectively, schools should include this and the following facts in the education of science.

1—Scientists have discovered over 30 parameters of physics that must be fine-tuned to an incredible degree of accuracy to support life on our earth. The odds of even one parameter of physics to accidentally happen with such accuracy of fine tuning is infinitesimally and unimaginably minute. Albert Einstein, Robert Jastrow, Fred Hoyle, and many other scientists say this indicates that there is an intelligent designer who planned and created the universe. —"Fine tuned universe"—Robbin Collins, PhD, pages. 130, 131,132 – "The Case for a Creator", Lee Strobel – 2004 Zondervan.

2—They have also discovered that dead matter cannot assemble itself into even one living cell because atoms and molecules are mixed and separated constantly in the earth's waters. Even if a few amino acids were to form, this would be far away from the necessary DNA. We also know that encoded DNA information can only come from a thinking mind. Again, the only way even one living cell can exist is through an intelligent designer – who is God. — "DNA information"—Stephen C. Meyer, PhD, pages 223, 224, 225 – "The Case for a Creator", Lee Strobel – 2004 Zondervan

3—Darwin said that if no proof of his long term "tree of evolution" was found before the Cambrian era, his theory would be invalidated. He also said that if the simplest living cell was irreducibly complex, it would be invalidated. One hundred and fifty years later, no long term "tree of evolution" leading up to the vast array of species of the Cambrian era has been found; and the simplest living cells have been found to be irreducibly complex. Concerning Darwin's "Origin of the Species", microbiologists have discovered that even the most primitive cells are irreducibly complex; this means that every molecule, biochemical and structure of any cell must be in place all at once for there to be life - thus life cannot have evolved. (See my additional comment about Darwin's theory below). For example: Let's say that one hundred amino acids miraculously formed in "a warm little pond"; they would not know how to reproduce, and thus they would simply disperse. Even if they formed a cell membrane, they would still not be a living cell and could not reproduce; therefore, they would decompose. Darwin's theory requires reproduction for evolution to occur. Under the problems stated above, there is just no way warm, dirty pond water could have accidentally evolved into a living cell.—"Irreducibly complex" Paraphrased from— Jonathan Wells PhD, pg. 43 - "The Case for a Creator", Lee Strobel – 2004 Zondervan, and Michael J. Behe, PhD, 197- "The Case for a Creator", Lee Strobel – 2004 Zondervan,

I have much more to say about Darwin's theory—

Darwin's Theory of the Origin of Species – as written by a modern scientist:
The first stage on the road to life is presumed to have been the build-up, by pure chemical synthetic processes occurring on the surface of the early Earth, of all the basic organic compounds necessary for the formation of a living cell. These are supposed to have accumulated in the primeval oceans, creating a nutrient broth, the so-called "prebiotic soup". In certain specialized environments, these organic compounds were assembled into large macromolecules, proteins and nucleic acids. Eventually, over millions of years, combinations of these macromolecules occurred which were then endowed with the property of self-reproduction. Then, driven by natural selection ever more efficient and complex, self-reproducing molecular systems evolved until finally the first simple cell systems emerged.

The following is My Critique of Darwin's Theory: This scientist's statements are italicized below and numbered 1 though 5.. My critiques have "My comment" with an arrow pointing to them:

Sentence 1 - *"The first stage on the road to life is *presumed to have been the build-up, by pure chemical synthetic processes occurring on the surface of the early Earth, of all the basic organic compounds necessary for the formation of a living cell."*

My comment > Note the word *"presumed" in this sentence. - A thing *presumed means nothing in a theory. It means Darwin was making guesses at a theory. A theory is when the author has a substantial amount of evidence to which he gives a believable explanation.

The idea of pure chemical synthetic processes occurring on the early Earth is ineffable twaddle. Why? There was almost always some degree of movement everywhere on the microscopic level; minute shifting, rising, stirring, by convection, breezes, flowing or vibration by rain or earthquakes—under a poisonous **atmosphere which scientists have recently found to have existed on early Earth. **atmosphere: Scientists now believe the "early Earth's" atmosphere at the time Darwin's chemical processes were supposed to have occurred consisted of carbon dioxide, nitrogen and water vapor. The atmosphere at that time was extremely toxic for life – at the least!

My comment> The last part of sentence 1 "...all these basic organic compounds" - if they ever did form, would have been poisoned and separated long before a single protein compound could have formed in such an atmosphere and conditions.

Sentence 2 - *These are *supposed to have accumulated in the primeval oceans, creating a nutrient broth, the so-called **"prebiotic soup".*

My comment> Imagine a dab or bucket of soup floating around in these oceans of the early Earth; it would have dispersed exceedingly rapidly – the pure chemical synthetic processes couldn't have formed a single amino acid. *supposed – this is an admission of guessing.

**Ahhh - the "poisoned prebiotic soup". This soup sounds, and is, absurd. Not one viable protein has ever been created under perfect conditions in a laboratory; and this theory is claiming that a chain of accidental combinations of just the right compounds could hold together in the poisonous, wind-blown, tossing, crashing waves, and the filling and flushing of the sloughs along the coasts of the primeval oceans of the early Earth mentioned in sentence two; not to mention the perpetual flow of the tides around the continents. The ocean water is also constantly moving because it is completely circulated every two years through the 800 degree volcanic vents running most of the length in the center of all the ocean bottoms.

This tremendous heat causes hot water to rise toward the ocean surface. Thus, the cold water at the bottom of the ocean is hydraulically sucked toward the vents. This, hydraulic suction is "felt" equally up to the continental shelves and shorelines on both sides of all the vents. These two effects create the two year circulation of the water in all the oceans. And this causes microscopic movement everywhere, including those areas with the broth of the prebiotic soup. This is another way these delicate, microscopic, would be compounds are dispersed into destruction.

Sentence 3 - *In certain specialized environments these organic compounds were assembled into large macromolecules, proteins and nucleic acids.*

My comment> The organic compounds would have already been poisoned and dispersed, thus the large macromolecules would not have had a chance to form at all. Any hint of a protein would have been fried by the carbon dioxide, nitrogen and water vapor in the atmosphere.

Sentence 4 - *Eventually, over millions of years, combinations of these macromolecules occurred which were then endowed with the property of self-reproduction.*

My comment> As I said above, these supposed combinations of macromolecules never could have existed due to the poisoned, shifting, flooding, tumultuous surface of early Earth. And, not only that, no property of a living cell, such as self-reproduction can be "endowed" to lifeless imaginary macromolecules in a "warm little pond". To invoke "endowment" of self-reproduction" is to admit they have no idea how self-reproduction spontaneously occurred out of nothing.

Sentence 5 - *Then driven by natural selection ever more efficient and complex self-reproducing molecular systems evolved until finally the first simple cell systems emerged.*

My comment> Sentence 5 touts "natural selection" when macromolecules are imaginary. Actually, it usually takes about 100 amino acids to form a protein molecule. This is far away from self-reproduction and is not possible without the simplest living cell in the first place. The simplest living cell has to have all its parts (thousands of them) put together all at the same time; and also must have an ancient ancestor that was created and sustained by God – for it to have life. No living things ever existed before God created them! .

So, as you can see, Darwin's "Origin of Species" is not a scientific theory. It is a myth or a wish list at best.(3)

NOTE: "The Origin of Species and the Descent of Man", the book by Charles Darwin got five stars from customer reviews on Oct. 16, 2016. Here is the leading quote "The Origin of Species" (1859); speaks to the "evolution" of species through "natural selection"...." These reviewers never ask this question: How did inert, lifeless chemicals, minerals, and various poisoned, simple molecules, in dirty water pop into life in the tumultuous, shifting, flooding, poisonous soil of the early Earth; or its surging, stirring, heaving, tumbling oceans?

The only evolution that exists are the changes we see that God makes in the living things He created in the first place. Since science has verified that God created the whole universe in a tremendous, magnificent, unimaginable series of events, scientists are not philosophically justified to assert that He could not have created life during the six days as told in the very brief synopses given in Genesis 1:1-26. Darwin's theory would be placed on the library shelves, so students could read this failed attempt at explaining the origin of life – it they wanted to.

Teaching the things mentioned above would inspire children to think about all the concepts of nature and of the Creator who is above, beyond, and greater than the universe.

The Great Stumbling Block:
Confusion and frustration can occur when an old concept clashes with a new one. Darwin's ideas may have been written to shut down Christianity—it certainly seems that way to millions of people. This conflict has created a stumbling block that harms hundreds of millions of people over the years because it turns away many of those who are future believers from living wonderful years believing in our God and Savior, Jesus Christ, until many years later.

Many scientists have worked very hard to find the origin of the universe and mankind. A great many of them have been honest and discovered things that help us against the myth of Darwinism. Below is some of the impressive discoveries?—

Mankind: Scientists have found a number of fossils that have characteristics very similar to ours and a great many "human skeletal remains that are up to 1.8 million years old". These ancient human type skeletal remains that have been found are adequately numerous and impressive, and combined with the fact that Chinese history is over six thousand years old, we must address these facts or lose millions more of our children to Darwinism and Satan. The geological record indicates that an early proto-man lived more than 2 million years before Adam was made in God's image. There had been many significant changes in proto-man by the Lord before He created Adam in the sixth day of creation. Archaeologists, as mentioned in chapter two, have found five beautiful Georgicus Dmanisi skulls and skeletal parts in a cave in Georgia, which is just eight hundred miles north of Southern Iraq (where the Garden of Eden is thought to have been). In my opinion the remains of proto-man such as those of Dmanisi Georgicus may have ancestors who were 2.4 million years old - (as humans and scientists perceive time). I can't say it enough.— We must end this Great Stumbling Block!

IMPORTANT STATEMENT: I have prayed for the past eight years. And I have meditated and searched for the answers to the statements in Genesis 1:1-26 for the past sixty-two years. Ironically, God has helped scientists to give us answers that solve very important conflicts between Genesis and Science.

NOTES

1   Quoted from Bill Nye to Newsmax TV: Evolution Denial 'Unique' to US - By Sean Piccoli | Tuesday, 09 Dec 2014 06:09 PM http://www.newsmax.com/Newsfront/bill-nye-evolution-denial-science/ 2014/12/09/id/612087/#ixzz4Dci8rHEZ

2   Quotes from Willian Lane Craig, PHD, THD - "The Case for a Creator" - pg. 106. "The Big Bang model has impressive scientific credentials".

4

ANSWERS CONSERNING GENESIS, SCIENCE AND CHRISTIANITY

GENESIS 4:16, 17 and 25 -
The Long Standing Question of Where Cain's Wife Came From:
By the time we get to Genesis chapter 4:16-19, Adam and Eve's two and only children were Cain and Abel. In the following verses God's word says that after murdering Abel, Cain left the presence of God and went east of Eden and took a wife in the land of Nod. (Cain must have taken a wife in the land of Nod because he and Abel were Adam's only descendants at the time). Hence, this indicates that proto-man already existed outside of the Garden of Eden as described above concerning Genesis 1:26. See Genesis 4:16, 17 and 25 below:

Verse 16 - "Cain went out from the presence of the Lord, and settled in the land of Nod, east of Eden". – [No other children were born to Adam and Eve when Cain left them].

Verse 17- "Cain had relations with his wife and she conceived and gave birth to Enoch…." – [Cain finds a wife in Nod and she was not born of Adam and Eve – see verse 25 below]:

Verse 25 – Adam had relations with his wife again; and she gave birth to a son, and named him Seth, for, *[Eve] said, "God has appointed me another offspring in place of Abel, for Cain killed him"*. [Because the story in verse 25 is after the events listed above, it must mean they gave birth to their third child, Seth, to replace Abel after Cain went to the land of Nod].

Was Cain's Wife His Sister?

There are some who will dispute my assertions about Cain taking a wife from outside of Adam's descendants: In a recent book on answers to the creation, it says the following: "...since it can be shown that there was plenty of time for a substantial population to be built up on Earth before Cain killed Abel—well over a hundred years"[1] This statement is unfounded! It is unfounded because nowhere in Genesis does it even imply that there was a substantial population built up before Cain went east of Eden. His departure reads as though it was immediately after he murdered Able. Genesis 4:25 clearly indicates that Adam and Eve had Seth after Cain had a son named Enoch. Please let me emphasize that Seth's birth is the only birth mentioned after those of Cain and Abel. And, according to the scriptures, there were other children born after Seth – but not before. Therefore, Cain did not marry his sister.

Leaving Eden and Entering the Wider World:

The scriptures found in Geneses 4:16, 17 and 25 point to a proto-man that was living in the wider world. Therefore, these scriptures most likely indicate that Cain took a contemporary member of proto-man to be his wife after he went to the land of Nod. (By that time God had physically "evolved" proto-man until they were physically similar to Adam, as seen in human skeletal remains from 7,000 to 400,000 years ago). The scientific proof that they existed is found in the yearly layers of the earth's continents and many other types of corroborating dating. This shows that proto-man existed even before two million years ago, as scientists understand time. Since they existed from that long ago, our interpretation is that God planned to end proto-man by changing them into "His image". He accomplished this when Adam's off-spring intermarried with them, and their children and descendants were changed into God's image – having a spirit, conscience, and eternal life if they believed in Jesus.

Some people have asked me this question:

"In Genesis 1:20-26 it says there were living creatures and God saw that it was good, so how could there have been animals dying before the fall?" My answer is this: In the _second half of the sixth day of creation_ God created Adam, and in Genesis 2:8 God created the Garden of Eden as a paradise for Adam, Eve, and all their descendants. Let's go back to the fifth day of creation where He had created many animals and told them to be fruitful and multiply. And by _the first half of the Sixth Day of creation, He had created everything that creeps on the ground._ All these animals were not in any kind of paradise, and they did not have a moral conscience, a spirit, and eternal life – like Adam. They were in a natural world where they had to struggle for their survival. Thus, in nature's cycles, these animals were compelled to die so that the earth would not get overpopulated with animals.—And, if some of the herbivores were not killed by predators they would have eaten too much of the vegetation and would have died of starvation in the winter— which would be bad. Also, the carnivores would have starved when too many of the herbivores died. This is the "balance of nature". We know there were carnivores by their numerous fossils and remains of herbivores that they killed because we find tooth marks on their fossilized bones. Herbivore bones are also found in the stomachs of carnivore fossils and remains. We also know proto-man killed and ate herbivores because we find spear points stuck in bones of herbivore fossils. The actions of carnivores are common knowledge to anyone who has studied archaeology. Now to finish my answer: Adam and Eve lived in a paradise named the Garden of Eden; which disappeared after the fall. These animals had always lived in the natural world, which was probably somewhat like it is today.

The earth has a certain amount of space; therefore, if there were no predators and the herbivores lived forever, the earth would have become over-run with these animals and the vegetation would have been stripped to the ground. Then all the animals would have lain down starving and yet would not die. Would God say this is good?

When the various animals died, they simply turned into skeletons if they were not eaten - and so did proto-man. Adam and Eve had eternal life, but they lost it when they disobeyed God and ate from the tree of good and evil. I notice in the scriptures that God placed Adam in a paradise called the "Garden of Eden". This set mankind apart from the wider world, and after the fall, the Garden of Eden vanished.

SCIENCE AND CHRISTIANITY-

I believe that sticking to the idea that science is only a philosophy is a big mistake. After all, the word philosophy means "the love of knowledge, truth, the nature and meaning of life, etc.", and most scientists believe in this - it is the main principle of their religion. The following is what Robert Jastrow said about this religion: "If these scientists really examined the implications of the universe being created out of nothing, they would be traumatized."2 By earnestly seeking the truth in God's natural world, many scientists have discovered a large number of undeniable things that God created.

Scientists convert to believers:

Scores of scientists, including Albert Einstein, Robert Jastrow, and Allan Sandage, became believers in God after the discovery that the universe appeared out of nothing and the scientific discoveries mentioned in Chapter1 and 2 of this book. Thus, they realized that what the Bible says is true. Cosmologist Jastrow said this, "Astronomers now find they have painted themselves into a corner because they have proven, by their own methods, that the world began abruptly in an act of creation to which you can trace the seeds of every star, every planet, every living thing in this cosmos and on the earth. And they have found that all this happened as a product of forces they cannot hope to discover.... That there are what I or anyone would call supernatural forces at work is now, I think, a scientifically proven fact."[2]

Why is mankind so often selfish and proud?

Before God made mankind in His image, every living creature fought for its own interests first and sometimes only, including proto-man. Proto-man must have had mental impulses which were selfish just like all the other living creatures do - this may be why we also are self-centered and struggle to obey God and our God given spirit's moral conscience. This is why we do not always like to obey God – and this is why Adam and Eve and all the rest of us commit sins.

CHRISTIANITY-

The foremost teaching of Christianity is to love God with all your heart. One who wants the righteousness of God will love Him because they know from His teachings that He will plant and increase righteousness in him/her by the Holy Spirit. Christians do not think they are righteous; they are seeking it with all their hearts—we know we are sinners who need God's help. The second foremost teaching is to love your neighbor as yourself. We are taught and seek love in our hearts. I mention love because if we know every scripture in the Bible, yet don't love others, we are nothing. Of course when one loves God, he has faith in our Lord and Savior Christ Jesus.

God sent Jesus to atone for our sins:

God created and loves us; thus, He understands that death is the one thing we dislike the most. However, He promised Adam and Eve that they would surely die if they ate from the "tree of good and evil" (thus they began to partake of the concepts and practices of "good and evil"). We are all like Adam and Eve and partake of good and evil; this is why we are also doomed to die. Thankfully, God has provided a way for us to be with Him forever. "Due to our being captivated by our sin, we have brought ourselves to a state of misery and mortality. God is so loving, merciful, understanding, and forgiving that He, in human form, suffered and died on the cross in our place—and offers us grace and salvation". Paraphrased from "The Pilgrims Progess" by John Bunyan – 1678.

God is a just God, and He had a dilemma:

Because of our disobedience we could not be with Him, yet He wanted to save us from our sins. However, He had told Adam he would surely die if he ate from the "Tree of Good and Evil". And, since all men are sinful like Adam and for justice to be done, God had to die in our place to redeem us from the death we caused by choosing to be sinful. But how could God die? He took on a perishable human body; thus, He appeared in human form as the man, Jesus, who was indwelled by the Father's Spirit. Hence, it was God's human form who died on the cross and was resurrected by the Everlasting Father. So, it is by His grace that we are saved when we have faith in Jesus, and He resurrects us after our human bodies die. Again, since God created the whole universe, He can surely resurrect our bodies so we can live and be with Him for eternity.

What is resurrection?

This is what the Apostle Paul says in 1 Corinthians 15: 40, 43, 40 "There are earthly bodies, and heavenly bodies, but the glory of the earthly is one, and the glory of the heavenly is another. The earthly is sown a perishable body; the heavenly is raised an imperishable body." 43 "It is sown in dishonor; it is raised in glory. It is sown in weakness; it is raised in power." 44 "It is sown a natural body; it is raised a spiritual body. If there is a natural body, then there is a spiritual body." Thus, we are raised a sacred, immortal, physical body and enter the kingdom of God.

Witnesses of the Resurrection who saw, touched, and spoke to Jesus:

The Apostle Paul in 1 Corinthians 15:1-11, wrote. 1 Now I make known to you, brethren, the gospel which I preached to you, which also you received, in which you also stand, 2 by which also you are saved, if you hold fast to the word I preached to you, unless you believe in vain. 3 For I delivered to you as of first importance what I also received, that Christ died for our sins according to the scriptures, 4 and that He was buried, and that He was raised up on the third day according to the scriptures, 5 and that He appeared to Cephas [Peter], then to the twelve. 6 After that He appeared to more than five hundred at one time, most of whom remain until now, but some have fallen asleep. 7 Then He appeared to James, then to all the apostles, 8 and last of all, as it were to one untimely born, he appeared to me also.

The Jewish leaders did not dispute that Jesus' tomb was empty; therefore, they were implicitly saying Jesus was crucified and buried in Joseph of

Arimathea's tomb! After Jesus appeared to all the people mentioned above, the apostles, Paul, and Jesus' brother, James, all of them boldly spread the gospel knowing Jesus had been crucified. They continued preaching even though they were threatened, stoned, beaten with the rod, stabbed with the sword, saw other apostles crucified, and John was jailed until he was ninety years old. "While most people can only have faith that their beliefs are true, the disciples were in a position to know without a doubt whether or not Jesus had risen from the dead. They claimed they saw Him, talked with Him and ate with Him. If they weren't absolutely certain, they wouldn't have allowed themselves to be tortured to death for proclaiming that the resurrection had actually happened. People will die for their religious beliefs if they sincerely believe they are true, but people won't die for their religious beliefs if they know their beliefs are false".—Quote from J. P Moreland, "The Case for a Creator", pages. 247, 248 – Lee Strobel – 1998.

Where does the Bible say we are resurrected with a physical body?
One place is Luke 24:39 and 41 where Jesus said to the eleven and those who were with them, "See My hands and My feet, that it is I Myself; for a spirit does not have flesh and bones, as you see that I have" - and verse 41 says, "...have you anything to eat?" Thus, after His resurrection, Jesus appeared to His apostles and disciples, He showed them His sacred, immortal, physical body and ate with them. This is the same type of body we will have after our resurrection—

The natural body is sinful and doomed to die; the spiritual body is sacred and imperishable. The word spiritual may lead some people to think we are raised as spirits, only. But the word spiritual means that which is sacred, and the word spirit means our personal spirit (that part of us which is our connection to God). Our personal spirit indwells our earthly body first, and then, it indwells our sacred, heavenly body when we are resurrected. How does He resurrect us? God has every person's DNA and RNA codes and everything else and simply transforms our perishable, earthly bodies into perfect, sacred, imperishable, heavenly bodies when we are resurrected and enter the kingdom of God.

NOTES

1   Quote from "The Creation Answer Book" pg. 137 - 2006
2   Astronomer, physicist and founder of NASA's Goddard Institute of Space Studies Robert Jastrow. See - Quotes about God to consider...if you think science leads to atheism ... Copy and paste on Google> godevidence.com/2010/08/quotes-about-god/ - Please see Jastrow's book God and the Astronomers for further reading.

5

HOW DID GOD CREATE
THE UNIVERSE?

For the past one hundred years scientific discoveries have supported the fact that the Bible says God caused the universe to appear upon His command out of nothing. And, to understand the magnitude of this supernatural event, we must grasp the fact that before God created the universe there was no matter, no energy, nor even the vacuum of space!

Who is This Transcendental Creator of the Universe?
There is just no way that the universe could have popped into existence out of nothing due to any known natural cause. Therefore, there must be an Intelligent Designer who created all the things in the natural world—such as the God who created the universe. God is the Creator of everything; therefore, He must have a Mind of tremendous power – the "Ultimate Mind".[1]

God is a personal Creator because He has His own volition or will. Science explains all phenomena in terms of the laws of nature. The following is a quote from William Lane Craig,

PHD, "If a man asks his wife, 'Why is the kettle boiling?' She might say, 'Well because the kinetic energy of the flame is conducted by the metal bottom to the water, causing the water molecules to vibrate faster and faster until, they're thrown off in the form of steam'. That would be a scientific explanation. Or she might say, I put it on to make a cup of tea.' That would be a personal explanation. Both are legitimate, but they explain the phenomenon quite differently". Therefore, God is a personal God who created the universe for His pleasure - and ours, yet, He is a Spirit with an immaterial, non-physical, Ultimate Mind. Science is, more and more, confirming what the Bible says about God and the universe.[2]

Let me quote again from Dr. Craig, PHD—"There cannot be a scientific explanation of the first state of the universe. Since it is the first state, it simply cannot be explained in terms of earlier initial conditions and natural laws leading up to it. So, if there is an explanation of the first cause of the universe, it has to be a personal explanation, that is, an agent who has volition to create it. That would be the first reason that the cause of the universe must be personal."[3]

Many scientists, including those who believe in an intelligent designer, say that the universe is immaterial. How can that be? The Bible gives us insight into how God created everything. Almost all of God's thoughts are, of course, incomprehensible to us. Again, the key to how God created everything is that He spoke the universe into existence. In John 1:14 He also tells us that the "Word", which is Jesus, is that part of God that created everything - and much more. "Word" in the Greek language is "Logos". "Logos" in English is "Concept"! Thus, our universe was created through physical concepts and spiritual concepts - with which God created everything. When we hear that everything was spoken into existence, what does that mean? Some people see the universe as accidental physical phenomena, only. However, scientists have discovered that everything in nature began to exist from a tiny dot in the center of the universe.3 This is impossible for what we call "natural" physics. It is above, beyond, and greater than the natural world. Therefore, it is not actually material! It is created by the transmission of informational concepts from God's Ultimate Mind to our minuscule minds.

My Thoughts and Three Experiences:

In the following paragraphs I will offer my thoughts on how God created everything in the universe. First I will give a few statements from the Bible and some of my observations that are the basis of my system of ideas that are intended to explain how God created the universe.—First and foremost, God said in Genesis 1:3 and 7: 3 "Let there be light"; and there was light. 7 "...and it was so" - which indicates He made all things by "speaking" them into existence with the power of His Mind and Spirit. Now my three experiences.[4]

1—Many people and I testify that we have had the following supernatural experience - to wit:: I have been looking at someone else who is twenty or so yards away when that person turns around and looks me in the eye, or someone is behind me and I turn around and look them right in the eye. There is no physical or technological device involved, so how do we know we are looking at one another?—It is done with the consciousness of each other through our spirits!

2—In 1983, I was headed home one evening from a one hundred and twenty mile trip in the dark with a fine drizzling rain. I was in the fast lane and another driver was following a bit too closely behind. I was aware that changing lanes was a main cause of most crashes on a freeway; therefore, I was very reluctant to change lanes. After several miles I heard a commanding voice say, "Change Lanes". I automatically flipped the turn signal, took a quick look, and changed lanes just in time to miss a pick-up truck laying on its side across the fast lane in the shadow of an overhead sign. I had changed lanes slowly and this must have allowed the tailgater to look past my car and see the truck in both our headlights. Thus, he saw the truck sooner than I would have. In my side mirror I saw he was stopping rapidly, and I didn't hear a crash, so he must have stopped. As I passed the pickup I saw three people behind the truck and over on the center emergency lane. There were houses close by, and I thought they could call an ambulance if needed. I believe that God communicated with me and saved my life—and the tailgater from being injured or killed by rear-ending me!

3—When I was twenty years old, I was working in my landlord's back yard removing some bricks and concrete blocks from the soil. While thinking about how the universe began, I stopped and decided I would try to visualize all the way out to the end of the universe. After several minutes I was in deep concentration far, far out and all of a sudden a small bright light appeared in the center of my vision, and it came toward me - enlaging quite rapidly. When it was right up to me, I shook my head in fear and opened my eyes. I was stunned! I was back in the yard! Now, it seems to me the light was from God to show me He was the origin of all things.

There are many other similar experiences like these that people have shared. One last word; I asked a friend, who is a physicist, if the following theory of how God created the universe is possible and he thought for a while and said – "Yes". Now, to my meditations and descriptions.—

How Does God Speak Everything into Existence?
Genesis 1: 1-26 indicates that God created everything before He created us. He took pleasure in it all. When I imagine God's mind, my ideas are, by comparison, minuscule and extremely simplified!—but, here goes. I have said that God's mind is the "Ultimate Mind" and thus He created our minds as "minuscule minds". His "Ultimate Mind" has a mental way of connecting, transmitting and receiving thoughts to and from our spirits. The transmission of thoughts to us is how He provides to us everything that we can experience and observe. His mind must have innumerable areas for the transmission of the various physical and spiritual (sacred) concepts into our minds. As I wrote in the paragraph above, in speaking things into existence as He states in Genesis 1: 3 and 7—verse 3 says, *"Let there be light"*, and verse 7 says, *"...and it was so,"*. Therefore, He must have areas for unimaginable thinking; storing all knowledge and remembering it all; imaging everything and programming all the things for each of our minds' senses; organizing; connecting things; consciousness of past, present, and future time. He has an area for each of our minds so we can receive our specific portion of the innumerable "physical" things He spoke into existence - and all the things He is sustaining and projecting to our minds and spirits on a continual basis. As we partake of these

experiences we can manipulate things with our physical bodies which are also transmitted to us.

Our minuscule minds:

How does He transmit His creations to our minds? The way God transmits the universe to our minds has the same exact details and clarity of everything that Darwinists, materialists, and naturalists describe as the natural world, and the perfection of these transmitted experiences our minds perceive are what I call "real things and events". Everything God transmits to us, we receive and interpret as the natural world because God transmits them perfectly to our five senses – sight, smell, taste, sound and touch. The following is the scientific description of how our five sense function; however I give the credit to God (in italics):

The receptors of these five senses pick up the characteristics of every transmitted phenomena they are exposed to and are sent to the brain and "interpreted":

1___*When God sends us light* - the eyes collect the light rays and when they strike either the rods or the cones of the retina; they are converted into an electric signal that is relayed to the brain via the optic nerve. The brain then "interprets" the electrical signals into the images a person sees.

2 ___*When God sends us odors* - the nose detects various odor molecules. Finally, they are released from the glomerulus and are interpreted in the brain as various smells.

3___*When God sends us flavors* – the tongue sends chemical information to the cerebral cortex and the brain interprets the sense of taste.

4___*When God transmits sound to* the ear – the cochlea gathers sound waves and sends nerve impulses to the brain where they are interpreted as sounds.

5___*When God transmits any kind of touch to us* - the body's touch receptors perceive sensations such as pressure, vibrations, texture, heat and cold and sends them to the brain where they are interpreted.

I noticed that none of these descriptions explain the mechanisms with which the brain interprets these sensations. I don't see how the brain could slowly evolve its ability to interpret these sensations, for example: how could the brain know what colors look like in the first place, so why would any brain have the first clue that there was any such thing as color? We cannot explain to a blind person how colors look. Therefore, the ability to "know" how to interpret the information from the receptor to recognize color, sound, smell, taste and touch would have undoubtedly been placed in our minds by our Creator.

Now, let me say a few words about God's universe and the imaginary universe of Darwinism and Materialism:
God's transmission of everything to our minds has the exact quality and details needed for the phenomena we experience. Since God's universe is the actual reality, the Materialists' concept of the universe is imaginary because they refuse to accept the newly found facts scientists have proven about the universe; and God's words in the Bible.

What are physical things?
The physical things are the things of the "natural world" and of the "heavenly world" that we receive from God and perceive with our eyes, ears, nose, tongue, body (touch), and our spirits (as described above). In other words, physical reality is what we can perceive with our senses and our spirits. There is no other way to know what is real in the physical, natural world, or in heaven, because all of the information each of us receives from God is marvelously and wonderfully coordinated, so we can experience the physical things of the world and of heaven. And, they obey the natural laws God has created. Thus, they are the created universe spoken into existence. They are concepts that are programmed, coordinated and projected to each of our minds and our spirits; therefore, it is what we perceive as absolute physical reality. Please let me quote Stephen C. Meyer, PHD. speaking on the "Big Bang" and Einstein's

"general relativity". "These two theories now point to a definite beginning of the universe. The fact that most scientists now believe that energy, matter, space and time had a beginning is profoundly anti-materialistic. You can invoke neither time, nor space, nor matter, nor energy, nor laws of nature to explain the origin of the universe. General relativity points to the need for a cause that transcends these domains."[5]

There are several sources which tell us that physical things are spoken into existence – God, our spirit, minds and senses. We perceive things that we think are physically "real" simply by using our five senses and our spirits. This makes them actual physical phenomena because they are absolutely real to us, for God created them perfectly and transmits them to our relatively "minuscule" but wonderful minds and spirits.

What are Spiritual things?
Spiritual means Sacred. Spiritual things are those that are venerated and associated with God and/or divine things – holy. These are the sacred things of God: His love, grace, righteousness, justice, compassion, mercy, faithfulness, forgiveness, morality, kindness and Holiness. God will help us achieve these things when we believe in Him and ask for them – of course, we will only be perfected in heaven. Some physical things are also sacred: our bodies are the Temple of God when we trust Jesus as our Savior and receive the Holy Spirit. And, concerning the resurrection of our physical body, Paul says in 1 Corinthians 15:44 "It is sown a natural body, it is raised a spiritual body". When we are resurrected, our heavenly bodies will be both spiritual and physical bodies!

I have mentioned "God" a number of times in this chapter. Now, I need to explain how Jesus is God. Thus, I would like to quote and paraphrase a very clear way of understanding how Jesus is God. I quote Michael Brown, PHD who said — "God is complex in His unity, and this One God makes Himself known as the Father, the Son, and Spirit....Interestingly, a Rabbi came up with a different concept about how He can be untouchable and invisible, yet touchable and known." One of the concepts was the Shekinah, which is the dwelling presence of God on Earth. God said in Exodus 25: 8 "Have them make a sanctuary for Me, and I will dwell among them."[6]

My Comments and a few scriptures:

Here are five, of many, verses that describe *the dwelling presence of God on Earth (Shekinah)* in the Bible:

1—Genesis 18: 1, 2, and 10 - verse *1 Now the Lord God appeared to him by the oaks of Mamre.... verse 2 ...behold, three men were standing opposite of him...and he bowed himself to the earth.* One of the three men was *the Shekinah – the dwelling place of God on Earth.* Thus God appeared to Abraham.

2—Exodus 3: 4 - verse 4 *God called him from the midst of the [burning] bush and said, "Moses, Moses!" And he said, "Here I am."* The Lord (God) appeared to Moses in "fire in the burning bush". The fiery bush was the Shekinah.

3—Daniel 3: 24, 25 - *"A fourth man in the furnace was 'a man like a Son of God'".* This fourth man was the Shekinah (God) in the furnace with Meshach, Shadrach, and Abed-nego. This was the Lord's appearance in Nebuchanazzer's furnace:

4—Exodus 40: 24,,34-38 – *a cloud by day and a fire by night.* This Shekinah was the Lord's presence in the tabernacle [ancient temple of the Jews]:

5—Phillipians 2: 8 says - *And (God) being found in the appearance of a man (Jesus), He humbled Himself...even [to] death on a cross.* God indwelled Jesus. Thus, Jesus was *the dwelling place of God on Earth* – the New Testament Shekinah!

"All things are possible with God". When we realize all the above concepts, this scriptural phrase makes more sense. This is how all things are possible with God. For example, He can say, "Let there be a physical particle one million times smaller than an atom" and it will appear, and then He can speak into existence a way for mankind to discover it - just like He has for all the other things scientists have discovered. And since God created the whole universe - He can certainly do far more than we can imagine.

CONCLUSION

Nine years ago I began writing an essay about the things I had read in Genesis chapters 1 through 4 and the things I read over the years about Darwinian evolution. A few years later I read Lee Strobel's books, "The Case for a Creator" and "The Case for Christ". While reading his books, I learned the universe just popped into being; thus it had to have a transcendental cause outside of nature that was eternal—which is God. By 2016 my essay had grown to forty-one pages and I decided to publish it as a small book so that young Christian high school and college students could be prepared for what their professors might try to teach them about Darwin's theories, even though they have thoroughly been proven false. I also want all Christians to be able to answer all the questions by people of any age who have been taught Darwinian evolution and Aristotle's cosmology of an eternal universe, which has also been proven erroneous. I don't mind if college professors teach scientific theories that are still considered plausible, but when they teach theories that have been thoroughly proven false, they need to be refuted—and Darwin's theories are being refuted by more and more scientists. Professors need to teach the up-to-date science and legitimate theories discussed in "The Case for a Creator"; and explain that these new discoveries have invalidated Darwin's theories. It would also be appropriate for public school books to mention the historic and scientific fact that Judaism and Christianity have stated for the past 3,200 and 2,000 years, respectively, that the universe was created out of nothing—no matter, no energy, nor even space!

Science has discovered the supernatural. For science to advance, this has to be admitted and researched in an honest manner, or science will lose its credibility. The New Testament gives us historical facts about Jesus – and there are many corroborating statements of this in the New Testament by historians; Josephus who lived from 37AD to 100AD and Tacitus who lived from 56AD to 120AD. Both were born during the time the Gospels were written. Many other historical corroborative statements were written just after Jesus' time and are also mentioned in "The Case for Christ". Compare Jesus' history to that of Alexander the Great, who died in 323BC and his biography was recorded four hundred years later by one source in 120AD. Few historians of today have a problem with how long it was until his biography was written – yet, it is considered very accurate. However, many present day historians try to discredit thirteen martyred eye witnesses' written accounts and dozens of other writers who lived at the same time as Jesus.

The purpose of this book is to inform young Christians, and others, who are in high school or college about Genesis, Science and Christianity, so they cannot be deceived by biased atheist professors, and for older people who have already been deceived by them, or the things of the world. It is also for Christians who are sharing the Gospel so they can make a defense to everyone who asks the difficult questions about the account of "creation" in chapters 1 through 4 in the Book of Genesis.

NOTES

1 The Ultimate Mind. Fred Hoyle, "The Case for a Creator", page 78 - 2004 - "a superintellect has...." 2 Quote from William Lane Craig, PhD, in "The Case for a Creator", - page 110 - 2004 - Zondervan - Lee Strobel. 3 Quote from William Lane Craig, PhD, in "The Case for a Creator", - page 110 - 2004 - Zondervan - Lee Strobel. 4 New American Standard Bible, Genesis 1:3 and 7. 5 Quote from Stephen C. Meyer, PHD., "The Case for a Creator", Lee Strobel, pg 77 – 2004.

2 Quote from William Lane Craig, PhD, in "The Case for a Creator", - page 110 - 2004 - Zondervan - Lee Strobel.

3 Quote from William Lane Craig, PhD, in "The Case for a Creator", - page 110 - 2004 - Zondervan - Lee Strobel.

4 New American Standard Bible, Genesis 1:3 and 7.

5 Quote from Stephen C. Meyer, PHD., "The Case for a Creator", Lee Strobel, pg 77 – 2004.

6 "The Case for the Real Jesus", Lee Strobel, pg. 205.

Printed in the United States
By Bookmasters